By Courtney Carbone

Random House 🏠 New York

Copyright © 2019 GoldieBlox, Inc. All rights reserved. Published in the United States by Random House Children's Books, a division of Penguin Random House LLC, 1745 Broadway, New York, NY 10019, and in Canada by Penguin Random House Canada Limited, Toronto. Random House and the colophon are registered trademarks of Penguin Random House LLC. GoldieBlox and all related titles, logos, and characters are trademarks of GoldieBlox, Inc.

Visit us on the Web!
rhcbooks.com
GoldieBlox.com

ISBN 978-1-9848-5153-6

Printed in the United States of America

10 9 8 7 6 5 4 3 2 1

GoldieBlox.

EVERYDAY DIY

20+ PROJECTS FOR MAKER GIRLS

CONTENTS

INTRODUCTION

What's up, Hackers?
Welcome to my DIY book!

I know what you're thinking. "Um . . . what? Goldie has an activity book now?"

Amazing, right?!

Seriously, I'm so excited to share these DIYs with you. This book has ALL MY FAVES from my YouTube show *Hack Along*, with lots of fun—and *functional*—projects and life hacks that will help you become a maker just like me.

Whether it's decorating your room, t[...]ow fashion ideas, creating gifts for friends and family, prepping for school, or playing around with slime— I've got a hack for that.

And don't worry if you haven't tried DIYs before. I'll explain everything you need to know! Making stuff is my superpower, and I've been doing it for as long as I can remember.

How do I do it? Check out the Needfinding section on page 14. Making is about more than just having fun. It's also a great way to learn new skills—and about yourself! You may find out you're awesome at something you've never even tried before.

But the most important thing? You've gotta be willing to get your hands dirty (or glittery)!

If you're looking for fun DIY projects, subscribe to my GoldieBlox YouTube channel.

youtube.com/goldieblox

STEM

Have you ever heard of STEM? No, not like the green part of a flower (though it is that, too!). STEM is actually an acronym with a very different meaning. Drumroll, please . . .

I often like to put ART in STEM to make it STEAM!

S = Science

T = Technology

E = Engineering

A = Art

M = Math

Now, what comes to your mind when you think of these things?

100 lb. textbooks full of wordy definitions?

Endless pages of assembly instructions?

Those mysterious extra buttons on your calculator? (Really, what *are* those?)

You have to think BIGGER! Science, Technology, Engineering, and Math make the world go around. And STEM is not only fun and exciting—it's also *everywhere*! From the bike you ride to the apps you play—even the machine this very page was printed on—everything is powered by STEM.

Think of it this way: learning how stuff works is like giving yourself a new superpower!

You could use your new skills to . . .

Design the world's tallest building.

Invent your own ice cream flavor.

Build an app . . . that can build its own app!

Discover a whole new planet.

Find a cure for hiccups.

The possibilities are endless when you keep an open mind. But you might be thinking, *Goldie, I've got class tomorrow. How am I supposed to change the world?* Well, first of all . . . finish your homework! (lol jk)

For real, though: don't let the fact that you're young stop you from *anything*! There are tons of ways you can begin making right now. Just turn the page! Well, not yet . . . I'm not quite done.

If you wanna keep making, this book is just the beginning. Try a new hobby, join a robot-building club, or take a class to learn more about what YOU want to do. Whether it's paper engineering, computer coding, or candy making—go crazy! All it takes to be a maker is a little curiosity.

NEEDFINDING

NEEDFINDING = Identifying a need or a problem, and designing your own solution to it.

Want to be a maker like me? Then let's get started!

Look around you right now. Do you think everything worth inventing has already been invented?

NOPE! Every day, people like you and me come up with brand-new things to make life easier, fix things that already exist, or just make the world more fun. Yes, the world is full of amazing technology and inventions, but there's SO much more we can do.

For example, has your phone ever died while you were on the go? Invent a bag that charges your phone while it's inside!

Or maybe you can't find your carry-on among the billions of other suitcases that look just like yours. Design your own homemade luggage tag that lights up with LED lights so you never have to look twice at baggage claim again!

The next time you think, *I wish this thing was different*, say to yourself, "I'm going to *make* it different, and here's how. . . ."

NEED 1

1. Find a problem and write it down.

_____

_____

_____

_____

_____

_____

_____

_____

2. Brainstorm ideas on how to fix it.

_____

_____

_____

_____

_____

Get Creative!

_____

_____

3. Choose your favorite idea and design it below!
   It doesn't have to be a perfect picture—just draw
   whatever helps you see the solution.

NEED 2

1. Find a problem and write it down.

_____

_____

_____

_____

_____

_____

_____

2. Brainstorm ideas on how to fix it.

_____

_____

_____

_____

_____

_____

_____

_____

3. Choose your favorite idea and design it below! It doesn't have to be a perfect picture—just draw whatever helps you see the solution.

Get creative!

NEED 3

1. Find a problem and write it down.

_____

_____

_____

_____

_____

_____

_____

Get creative!

2. Brainstorm ideas on how to fix it.

_____

_____

_____

_____

_____

_____

_____

_____

**3. Choose your favorite idea and design it below!
   It doesn't have to be a perfect picture—just draw
   whatever helps you see the solution.**

TOOL KIT

Have you ever started wrapping a present, only to realize you don't have tape or scissors nearby? Having all your tools in one place makes life much easier! That's where your tool kit comes in. . . .

Every hacker needs her own personalized tool kit. Ready to get started?

1. First, get yourself a toolbox. Don't have one handy? Think again! Grab an old lunch box, a shoebox, or a plastic bin.
2. Empty out the box.
3. Customize the outside. You can use glitter, sequins, colorful duct tape, markers, stickers—whatever you want! I like to use cheetah-print tape and gold heart stickers.

4. Put your name on the outside of the box. Use letter stickers or permanent markers. You gotta let the world know it's YOUR toolbox.

5. Customize the inside. We all have a different way of organizing, so you do you, but I personally LOVE using silicone cupcake liners or Tupperware containers for very small items.

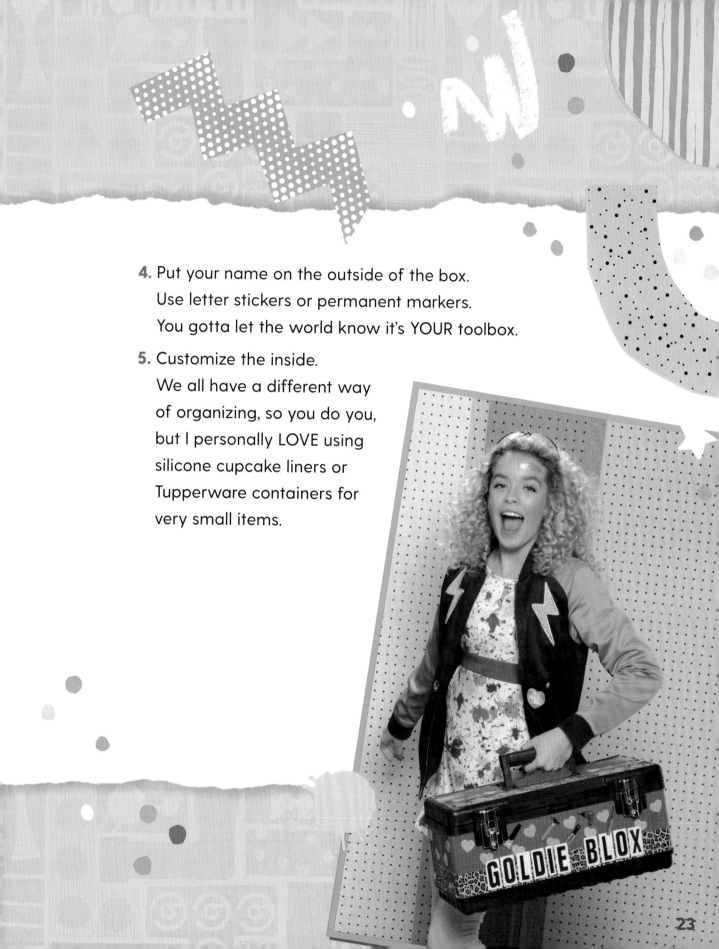

GOLDIE BLOX

Here are all the supplies I keep in my toolbox. I know. It's a LOT! But don't worry—you can build your supply over time. You may already have a lot of these items if you look around your house.

SAFETY GEAR
- ❑ Safety goggles
- ❑ Gloves
- ❑ Flashlight

Be extra careful whenever you're making stuff. Safety first!

TOOLS
- ❑ Screwdriver & screws
- ❑ Hammer & nails
- ❑ Wire cutters & wire
- ❑ Pliers
- ❑ Hot-glue gun

Get an okay—or a hand—from an adult before using these!

THE BASICS
- ❑ Scissors
- ❑ Ruler
- ❑ Duct tape
- ❑ Clear tape
- ❑ Glue or glue stick
- ❑ Rubber bands
- ❑ Sewing kit

Keep your scissors on top. Trust me, you'll use them a LOT!

Hair elastics can also work in a pinch!

CREATIVE SUPPLIES
- ❏ Markers
- ❏ Crayons
- ❏ Colored pencils
- ❏ Pens
- ❏ Paintbrush & paints

You can mix and match arts and crafts supplies. A handful of random supplies will work just fine!

DECORATIONS
- ❏ Ribbon
- ❏ Sequins
- ❏ Glitter
- ❏ Stickers
- ❏ Colorful tape
- ❏ Buttons

Don't have these around? Improvise with other things around your house. For example, paper cutouts from a three-hole punch make great confetti!

One last thing: don't forget to give your tools a fun nickname! They love it when you do that. Say what's up, Felicia? Ready to drill?

Piggy bank almost empty? No problem!

See what you already have lying around. (But make sure to ask before you take things that aren't yours!)

Have a lemonade stand to raise funds.

Visit your nearest dollar store. Mine is my favorite place ever, and a little goes a long way!

Check out garage sales in your neighborhood.

Collect old swatches of wrapping paper and fabric.

Cut out borders, pictures, and words from old magazines as decorations.

Have a stuff swap with friends (trade stickers, ribbons, buttons, etc.).

Clean out your closet and under your bed. You might be surprised by what you find. I know I always am!

Time to hack your world!

These DIYs are organized into five categories: Room Decor, Fashion, Gifts, Slime, and School. Each activity includes a cool STEM fact about the science behind it. And look for a golden lightning bolt to see how you can "Goldify" your hack to make it special!

MAKE STUFF AWESOME

YOU GOT THIS

SODA BOTTLE LIGHTS

Make recycling beautiful!

MATERIALS
- ❏ Plastic soda bottles
- ❏ Spray paint
- ❏ Colorful tape
- ❏ String lights

1. Cut a plastic soda bottle in half.

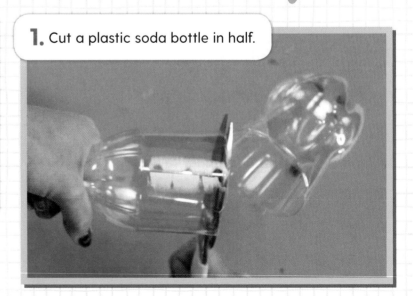

2. Cut into the upper half of the bottle to form a petal pattern.

3. When you're finished cutting out the petal pattern, start peeling the petals back.

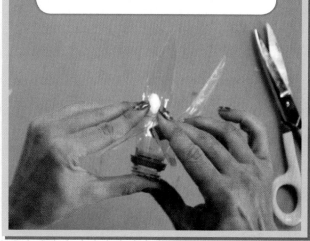

4. Press the petals down on a flat surface so they stick out.

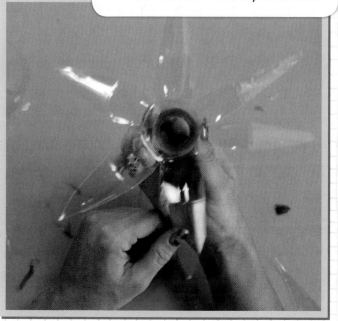

5. Repeat steps 1–4 until all your soda bottles look like flowers.

6. In a well-ventilated area, decorate your flowers with colorful spray paint. Let them dry.

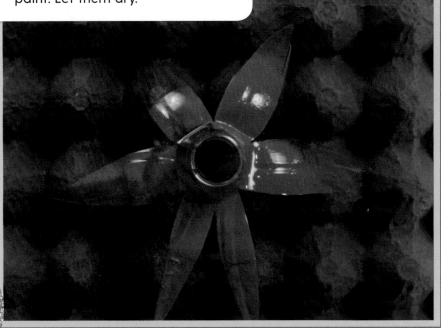

7. Apply two layers of colorful tape to the top of the bottle.

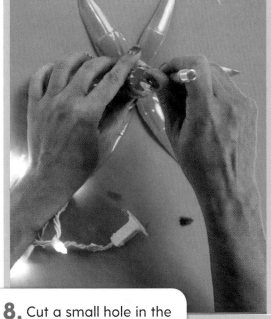

8. Cut a small hole in the middle of the tape.

9. Insert a string light through the hole in the tape.

10. Repeat steps 7–9 with the rest of your bottle flowers.

In 2014, Americans bought over 100 billion plastic drink bottles. That's 315 bottles per person! Most are never reused.

Your soda bottle lights can be used for any holiday. Make some scary monster mouths for Halloween or heart shapes for Valentine's Day!

PHONE-CHARGING STATION

I love this hack. It's stylish and practical and keeps your charging cord from flipping and flopping all over the place.

MATERIALS

❏ Empty shampoo bottle with enough room inside to hold your phone

❏ Felt

❏ Hot glue

❏ Trim

1. Draw an outline of where you want to cut the shampoo bottle. It should be deep enough to hold your phone and include a cutout square that's a little larger than your charger.

2. Cut the shampoo bottle into the shape of your phone-charging station.

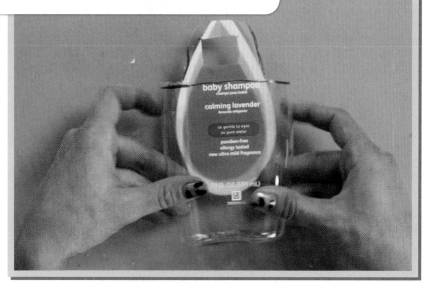

3. Cut out pieces of felt to line both the outside and inside of the shampoo bottle.

4. Cover the bottle with hot glue.

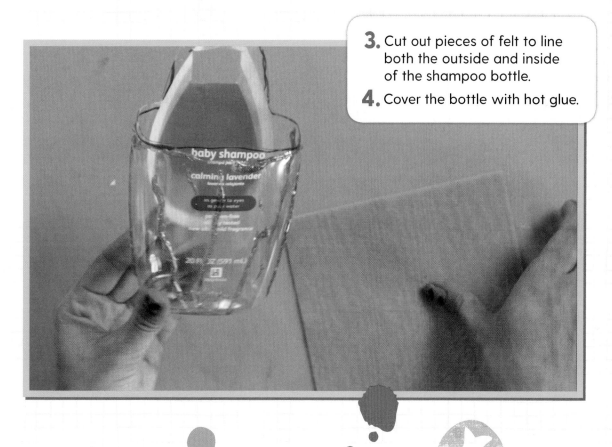

5. Apply the felt to the outside of the bottle.

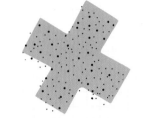

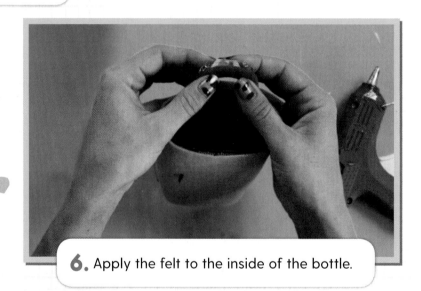

6. Apply the felt to the inside of the bottle.

7. Decorate your bottle with trim.

8. Hang the charging station on your charger and plug it into a wall socket. Attach your phone, and let electricity do the rest.

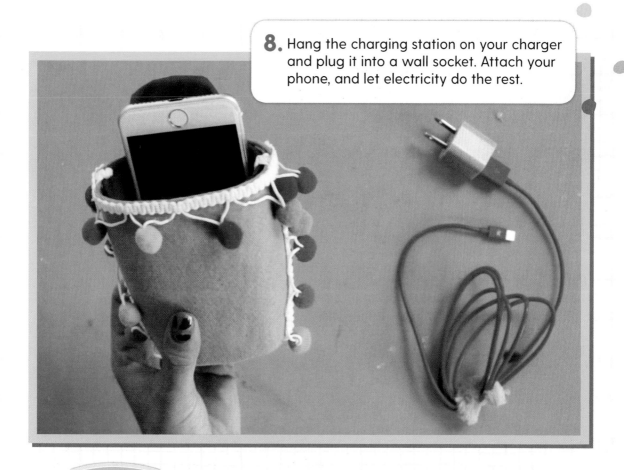

Normal power cables are like two-way streets: one wire brings electricity to the device and one sends it back. USB cables have two superthin wires for electricity *and* two for data. Gentle!

Want to make it more personal? Sew a funny patch or sequined appliqué to the front so everyone knows whose phone it is!

GLOW PILLOW

Okay, I gotta confess—
I still don't like to sleep
in a completely dark room.
A glow pillow is the perfect,
squishable solution!

MATERIALS

❏ 2 sheets of fluffy fabric
❏ Felt
❏ Hot glue
❏ Stuffing
❏ LED light
❏ Velcro

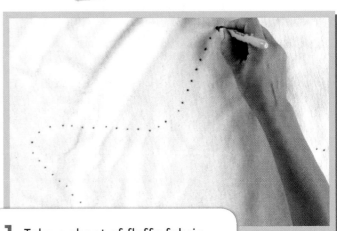

1. Take a sheet of fluffy fabric
and turn it onto its non-fluffy
side. Make an outline of a star.

2. Cut out your star. Then cut out another star the same size from your second piece of fluffy fabric.

3. Make a face using pieces of felt, and glue it onto one of your stars.

4. Cut a small slit in the middle of the other star. This is where you will insert your stuffing and your light.

5. Line up your two stars and glue them together.

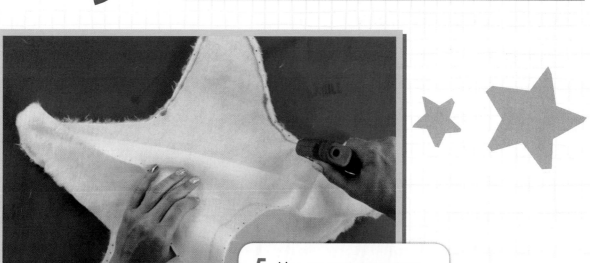

6. Add stuffing until your star pillow is nice and plump.

7. Turn on your LED light and insert it into your pillow.

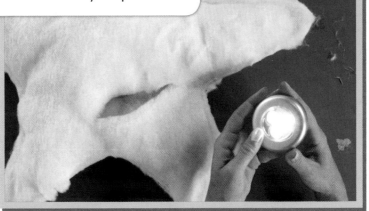

8. Glue pieces of Velcro along the slit so you can close up the hole.

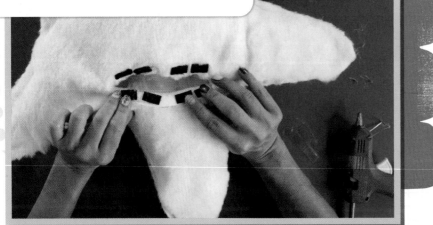

9. Watch your new pillow light up the room!

Compact fluorescent light (CFL) bulbs and older lightbulbs are like tiny space heaters, releasing more heat than light. Light-emitting diode (LED) bulbs emit 1/10 the heat of CFLs, so they make a much cooler pillow (and they don't shatter!).

There are lots of ways to remix this hack. Mix up the fabrics, textures, and shapes of your pillows to make your own fluffy pillow palace!

DRINK UMBRELLA LANTERN

Add a splash of color to your room!

MATERIALS

- ❏ Paper lantern
- ❏ Box of paper drink umbrellas
- ❏ Hot glue
- ❏ Small pom-poms
- ❏ Small lantern light

1. Open the paper lantern and rest it on a bowl so it doesn't move.

2. Open the drink umbrellas.

3. Cut the toothpick stem off each of the umbrellas.

4. Glue an umbrella onto the lantern.

5. Continue to glue umbrellas onto the lantern until it is fully covered.

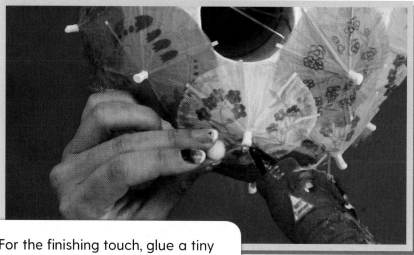

6. For the finishing touch, glue a tiny pom-pom onto each umbrella tip.

7. Place the lantern light inside the lantern. Hang it up, switch it on, and enjoy your colorful new creation!

STEM

You might think that covering a lantern with paper umbrellas would block the light, but it doesn't because the paper is translucent, or slightly see-through, which allows the light to pass through. So no worries—you can cover to your heart's content and create a colorful glow to your space.

Try gluing autumn-colored decorative leaves to your lantern for an outdoorsy look.

GLOW SHOES

Light up the streets!

MATERIALS

- ❏ 2 oz. glow powder
- ❏ 5 oz. clear glue
- ❏ Pair of white shoes

1. In a small bowl, combine the glue and the glow powder.

2. Mix until they are completely blended.

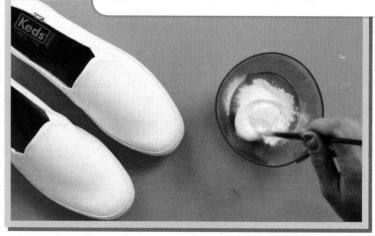

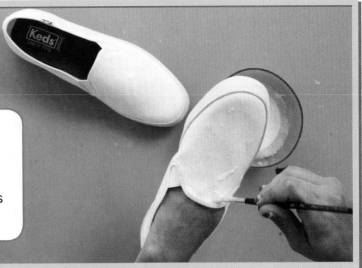

3. Paint any part of your shoes that you want to glow in the dark.

4. Add a second coat if you have enough mixture, and let your shoes dry overnight.

5. Shine a flashlight on your shoes for a few seconds—or just leave them out in the sun for a few minutes.

6. Turn off the lights and watch your shoes shine!

Phosphors absorb the energy from light and gradually release it, even in the dark. They're used to brighten CFL bulbs. That's why it sometimes takes CFLs a minute to get to full brightness.

If you want to add some flair to your shoes, get different glow-paint colors and make your own glow-in-the-dark designs!

FIREWORK NAILS

It's a fashion explosion!

MATERIALS
- ❏ Black nail polish
- ❏ Small brush
- ❏ Acrylic paints
- ❏ Clear top-coat nail polish

1. For a base coat, paint your nails with black nail polish.

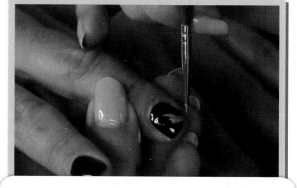

2. As soon as the polish dries, use your small brush and the acrylic paint to add small starbursts to your nails. Paint with short, quick strokes. Use whatever colors you want.

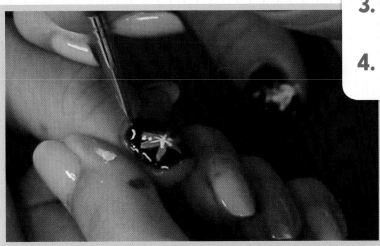

3. Once your nails are dry, make another starburst layer using white acrylic paint.
4. Add tiny white dots to the tips of each starburst.

5. Add a clear top coat.
6. Let the top coat dry. Now you're ready to celebrate!

STEM

The main ingredient in nail polish is nitrocellulose, a mix of wood fiber and the explosive in TNT! It's also in the glue that holds rows of staples together.

Nail art is great for any time of the year. Try painting flowers for spring, leaves for fall, snowflakes for winter, or atoms and molecules for a science fair presentation!

WAFFLE NECKLACE

Waffles are my absolute favorite food. Do I want to wear a waffle necklace 24/7? Yes, please!

MATERIALS

- ❏ Modeling putty and hardener
- ❏ Cornstarch
- ❏ Eye pin
- ❏ Red, blue, and yellow foam clay
- ❏ Varnish
- ❏ Brown paint
- ❏ Necklace chain

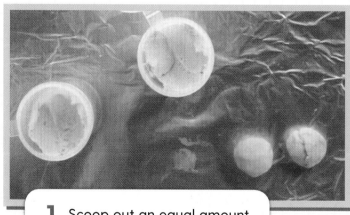

1. Scoop out an equal amount of putty and hardener.

2. Knead them together to form a ball one inch in diameter.

3. Flatten the ball into a two-inch disk.

4. Make a crisscross waffle pattern on the disk. You can use a ruler, a file, or anything else with a straight edge.

5. Cut out a square from your disk and let it harden.

6. Knead together a second ball of putty and hardener. Flatten it into a disk that will be the size of your necklace.

7. Add cornstarch to the waffle mold.

8. Squish the waffle mold down onto your disk.

9. Peel off the mold. You should have a delicious waffle pattern on your disk.

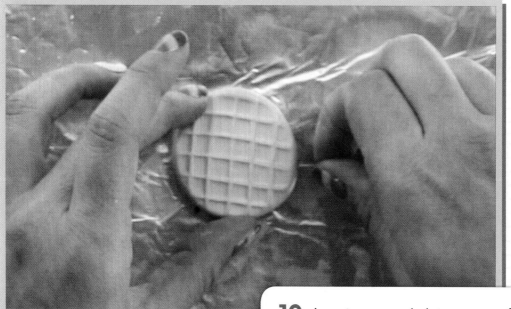

10. Insert an eye pin into your waffle.

11. Make your waffle toppings from the foam clay. You can roll out strawberries, blueberries, and butter pats!

12. To make the maple syrup, mix a small amount of varnish with a tiny amount of brown paint.

13. Place your toppings on your waffle.

14. Coat the toppings with the colored varnish.
15. Let your masterpiece dry overnight.

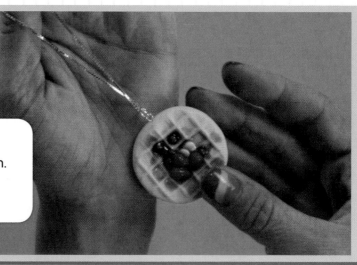

16. Thread your necklace chain through the loop in the eye pin. Voilà! You have one drool-worthy fashion accessory.

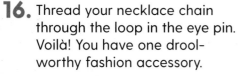

More than four thousand years ago, people were pouring boiling metal into molds to make spearheads and sculptures. Today, people inject plastic into molds to make everything from toys to machine parts.

Go wild with your toppings. Bananas? Yeah! Jalapeños and caramel? Double yeah! Cornflake peanut butter bacon waffles? Triple yeah!

FIDGET SPINNER

For the friend who can't stop, won't stop fidge-fidge-fidgeting!

MATERIALS
- ❑ Gold spray paint
- ❑ 5 plastic bottle caps
- ❑ Gold glitter hot glue
- ❑ 5 hex nuts
- ❑ Ball-bearing spinner

1. Paint your bottle caps gold.

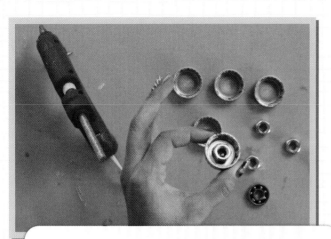

2. Glue the hex nuts into the bottom of the caps. This will help weigh the caps down and make them spin better.

3. Glue the caps to the ball-bearing spinner.

4. When you're done, the caps should completely surround the ball-bearing spinner.

5. Fill the gaps between the ball-bearing spinner and the caps with your gold glitter hot glue. If you just have regular glue, that's fine, too!

6. Hold the fidget spinner between your thumb and ring finger with one hand, and give it a whirl with the other. Now, that's what I call satisfying!

Ball bearings trap rolling balls between a wheel and an axle. That way they will never rub! Skateboards, cars, trains, planes, washing machines, and disk drives would not be possible without them.

Does your friend like a little extra oomph? Bedazzle the fidget spinner with jewels and sequins to make it extra fancy!

57

BATH BOMB GEODES

The perfect gift for the friend who's bubbly and fun!

MATERIALS

- ❏ 1/2 cup baking soda
- ❏ 1/4 cup citric acid
- ❏ 1/4 cup cornstarch
- ❏ Essential oils
- ❏ Rubbing alcohol
- ❏ Coconut oil
- ❏ Round soap mold
- ❏ Epsom salts
- ❏ Food coloring

1. In a bowl, mix together the baking soda, citric acid, and cornstarch.

2. Add a few drops of essential oils.
3. Add just enough rubbing alcohol so the mixture begins to clump.

4. Rub coconut oil over the inside of the soap mold.
5. Evenly press the mixture into both sides of the mold and let it dry.
6. Add a layer of Epsom salts to the soap mold.

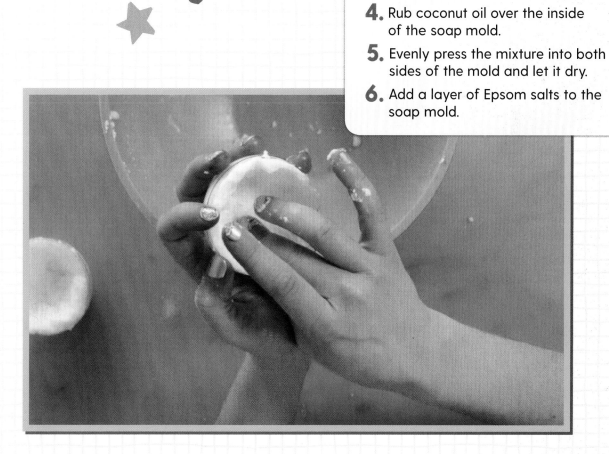

7. Fill a small bowl with more Epsom salts and add a few drops of food coloring.

8. Fill the rest of the soap mold with the colored Epsom salts. If you want, add some plain Epsom salts around the mold rims for texture.

9. Melt a few teaspoons of coconut oil and pour it over your mixture.

10. Let it cool in the fridge.

11. Use a spoon to gently pry the bath bomb geode out of the soap mold.

Oops! I packed this geode too tight.

It's really not coming out.

But you know what? That's okay. Making mistakes is all part of the journey!

If these geodes are too pretty to plop in a bath, keep them around as decorations instead!

STEM

How do bath bombs create all that fizzy goodness? The warm water mixes the citric acid and baking soda together, causing them to react. This chemical reaction creates carbon dioxide bubbles in the water—so soothing!

MAGNETIC CHECKERS

Want to reeeaallly have some fun with your friend? Play a game upside down!

MATERIALS

- ❏ Cookie sheet
- ❏ Tape
- ❏ Colorful acrylic paint
- ❏ Acrylic sealant
- ❏ Hot glue
- ❏ 24 magnets
- ❏ 24 toy pieces that can be turned into checker pieces (two different colors)
- ❏ Trim

1. Create an 8 x 8 grid on the cookie sheet, with each square measuring one inch.

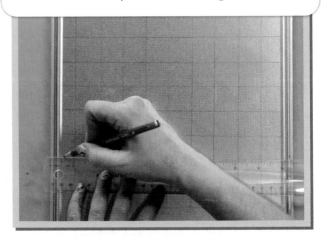

2. Tape off the edges of the grid.

3. Paint over every other square.

4. Remove the tape.

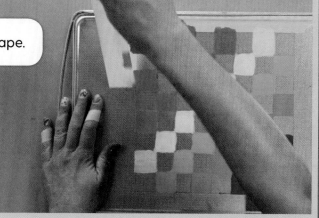

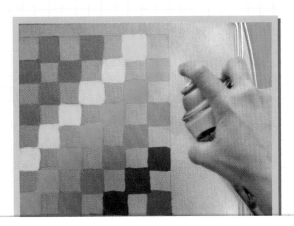

5. Spray acrylic sealant over your checkerboard.

6. Hot glue the magnets to the bottom of your toy pieces.

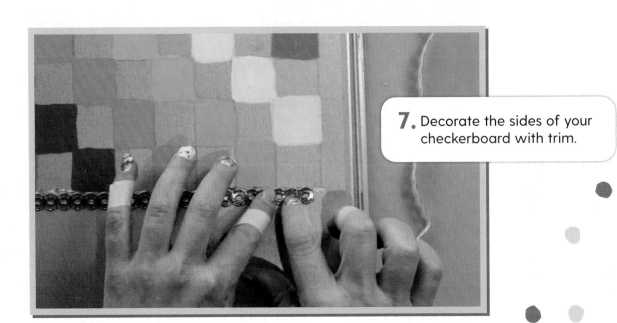

7. Decorate the sides of your checkerboard with trim.

64

8. Place the magnetic checker pieces on the board.

9. Check . . . it out!

There are 500 quintillion (500,000,000,000,000,000,000) possible moves in checkers. That's more than all the stars in the sky, grains of sand on Earth, or gallons of water in the ocean.

Do this hack as a chessboard and glue your chess pieces to magnets. That makes *two* games you can play with your bestie!

ROCK CANDY

Does your friend have a sweet tooth? Then there's no better gift than one made of PURE SUGAR!

1. Bring two cups of water to a boil.
2. Add five cups of sugar and stir until the sugar is completely dissolved.

MATERIALS

- ❏ 5 cups sugar, plus a little extra
- ❏ Food coloring
- ❏ Wooden skewer
- ❏ Mason jar
- ❏ Paper towel
- ❏ Clothespin
- ❏ Rubber band

3. Remove from heat and cool for ten minutes.

4. Pour the mixture into a bowl and mix in a few drops of food coloring.

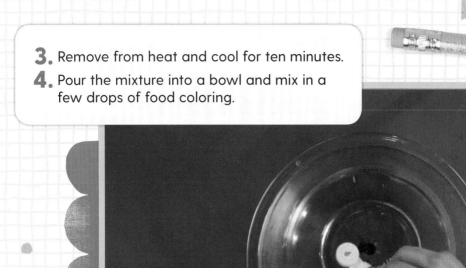

5. Dip one end of the skewer into the mixture.

6. Roll the wet end of the skewer in a bowl of sugar to form a base.

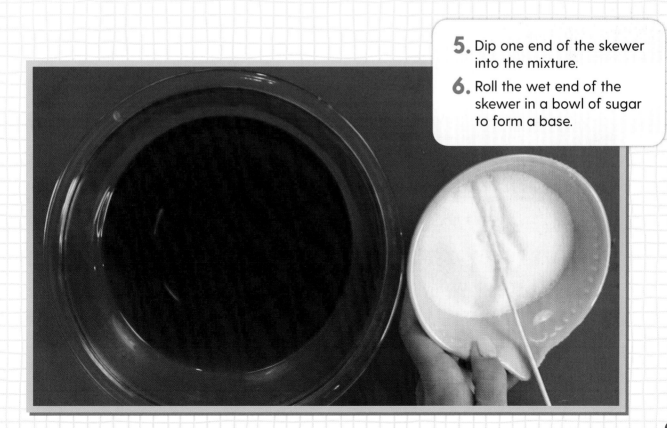

7. Carefully pour the mixture into the mason jar.

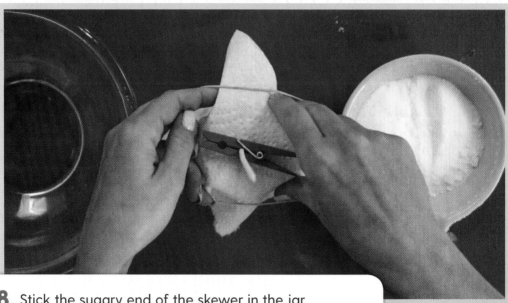

8. Stick the sugary end of the skewer in the jar.

9. Cover the jar with a paper towel. Attach a clothespin to the skewer to keep it upright and in the center.

10. Wrap a rubber band around the neck of the jar to secure the paper towel.

11. Let the jar sit for at least a week.

12. Remove the paper towel and clothespin.

13. Carefully pull out the most incredible piece of homemade rock candy ever!

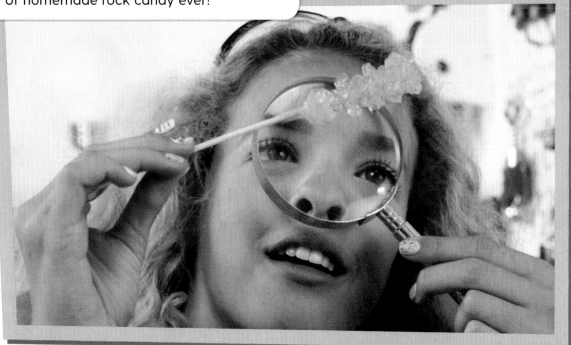

Each rock candy crystal has nearly a QUADRILLION molecules stuck to it. That's a lot of zeros!

Tie a ribbon around the bottom of the skewer to make it an extra-fancy gift!

SOAP GEMS

It's a cool gem!
It's colorful soap!
It's . . . both!

MATERIALS

- ❑ 2 lbs. clear soap
- ❑ Essential oils
- ❑ Silicone round mold with eight rounds
- ❑ Soap coloring
- ❑ Large silicone rectangular mold

1. Melt one pound of clear soap.

2. Stir in a few drops of essential oils.

3. Pour the soap into the round mold and mix in different colors with your soap coloring. Let the soap harden.

4. Remove the soap from the mold.

5. Chop the soap into rough pieces.

6. Place the rough soap pieces inside the rectangular mold.

7. Melt the other pound of clear soap and pour it into the rectangular mold. Let it harden.

8. Remove the soap from the rectangular mold.

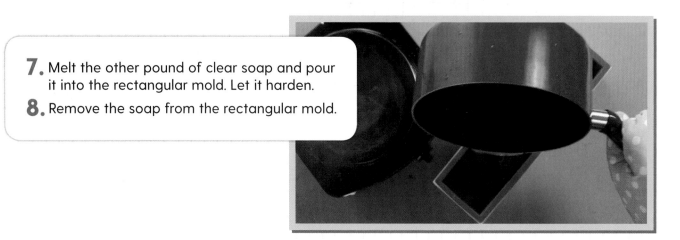

9. Cut the soap into rectangular blocks.

10. Cut up the soap to look like a gem.

Even though we're melting, mixing, and molding, there are no chemical changes in this hack. Scientists call these physical changes. Experiment with bits of soap, crayons, or colorful spices!

Why stop at gems? You can carve colorful cats, puppies, hedgehogs, rainbows, double rainbows or your very own creative art with this soap.

74

GOLD SLIME

Slime in my favorite color? I'm in!

1. In a medium bowl, mix the clear glue with 1/2 cup of water.
2. Add the contact lens solution.

MATERIALS

- ❏ 10 oz. clear glue
- ❏ 1/4 cup contact lens solution
- ❏ 1/4 cup gold pigment
- ❏ 1/8 cup baking soda

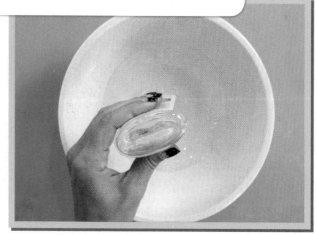

3. Add the gold pigment and mix well.

4. In a separate bowl, mix one cup of hot water with the baking soda. Let it cool.

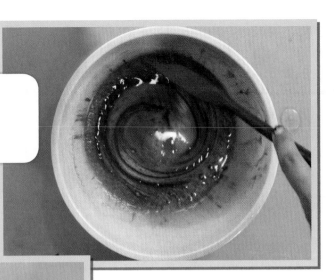

5. Slowly pour the baking soda solution into the gold mixture. Stir until you get the consistency of slime.

PURE GOLD!

Slime is a non-Newtonian fluid, which means it has characteristics of both a solid and a liquid. Scrunch slime in your hands and it looks like a solid ball. Open your hand and let the slime ooze between your fingers like a liquid. Mind officially blown!

It's no secret I'm a big fan of gold, but you can create slime in any color! Just substitute a different pigment. If you want extra-sparkly slime, try adding multicolor glitter to the mix!

COLOR-CHANGING SLIME

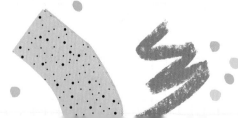

Watch your slime transform!

MATERIALS

- ❏ 5 oz. clear glue
- ❏ 1 Tbsp. heat-sensitive pigment
- ❏ 1/4 cup laundry detergent
- ❏ Liquid starch

1. In a medium bowl, mix the glue and the heat-sensitive pigment until well combined.

2. Slowly drizzle in the laundry detergent.

3. Add a few dashes of liquid starch and mix until you have the consistency of sticky dough.

4. Knead the slime with your hands until it's stretchy and soft.

5. To test out the color-changing properties, try dipping your slime in ice water or laying it against an ice cube tray for a few seconds.

STEM

Heat-sensitive—or thermochromic—pigment is the star of this slime. When the temperature changes, the crystals in the pigment move and change the spacing between them. This causes light to refract, creating different colors. The same material is found in mood rings and some lipsticks!

Make this hack a science experiment! Grab a thermometer. Fill some bowls with water of different temperatures and figure out the exact temperature that will cause your slime to change color.

EDIBLE SLIME

Ooey, gooey, and delicious!

1. Melt the coconut oil and marshmallows in a saucepan over medium-low heat.
2. Add the candy corn and stir until melted.

MATERIALS

- ❏ 2 Tbsp. coconut oil
- ❏ 1 cup marshmallows
- ❏ 1 cup candy corn
- ❏ 1/4 cup cornstarch
- ❏ 1/4 cup powdered sugar

3. Continue stirring and heating the mixture until it has the consistency of sticky slime.

4. On a plate, mix together the cornstarch and powdered sugar. Incorporate the powdered mixture into the slime. (This will make it less sticky.)

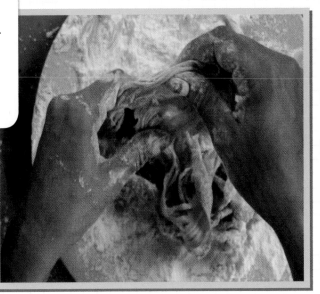

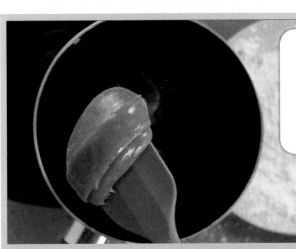

5. Return the slime to the saucepan and gently heat until the powdered mixture is fully absorbed.

6. Let the slime cool. Then enjoy your edible slime!

STEM

This slime is gooey and tasty, but it isn't the only edible material that flows like liquid and sticks together like a solid. Peanut butter, ketchup, honey, and cream are all non-Newtonian fluids.

Make some cool shapes with your edible slime while it's still soft. Then when it hardens, you've got yourself some delicious candy treats!

GLOW-IN-THE-DARK SLIME

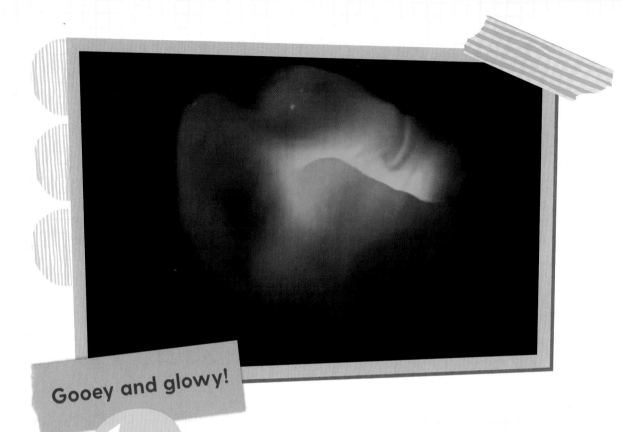

Gooey and glowy!

1. In a medium bowl, combine one cup of water with the clear glue.

2. Add the glow-in-the-dark paint and mix well.

MATERIALS

❏ 4 oz. clear glue

❏ 3 Tbsp. glow-in-the-dark paint

❏ 1/2 cup liquid starch

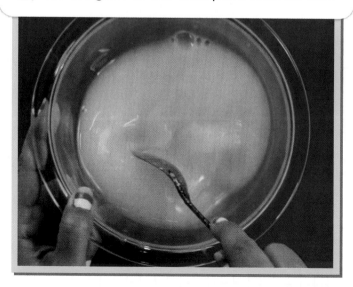

3. In a separate bowl, combine 1/3 cup of water with the liquid starch.

4. Stir the glue mixture constantly while slowly adding the starch solution to it.

5. Mix the slime until it resembles sticky dough.

6. Knead the slime with your hands until it's soft and stretchy. The more you knead it, the more rubberlike it gets!

7. Shine a flashlight on the slime for a few seconds to charge it. Then turn off the lights and watch it glow!

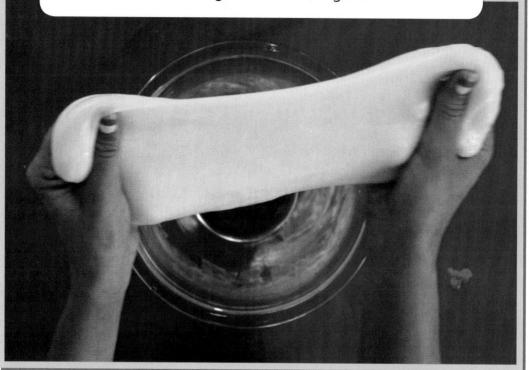

Like plants, your glow-in-the-dark slime needs sunlight. Anything that glows in the dark contains a substance called phosphors. Exposing phosphors to light energizes them, and that stored energy is slowly released, creating small amounts of light.

Add some aliens or monsters to your glowing goo for a cool, creepy scene!

SCHOOL

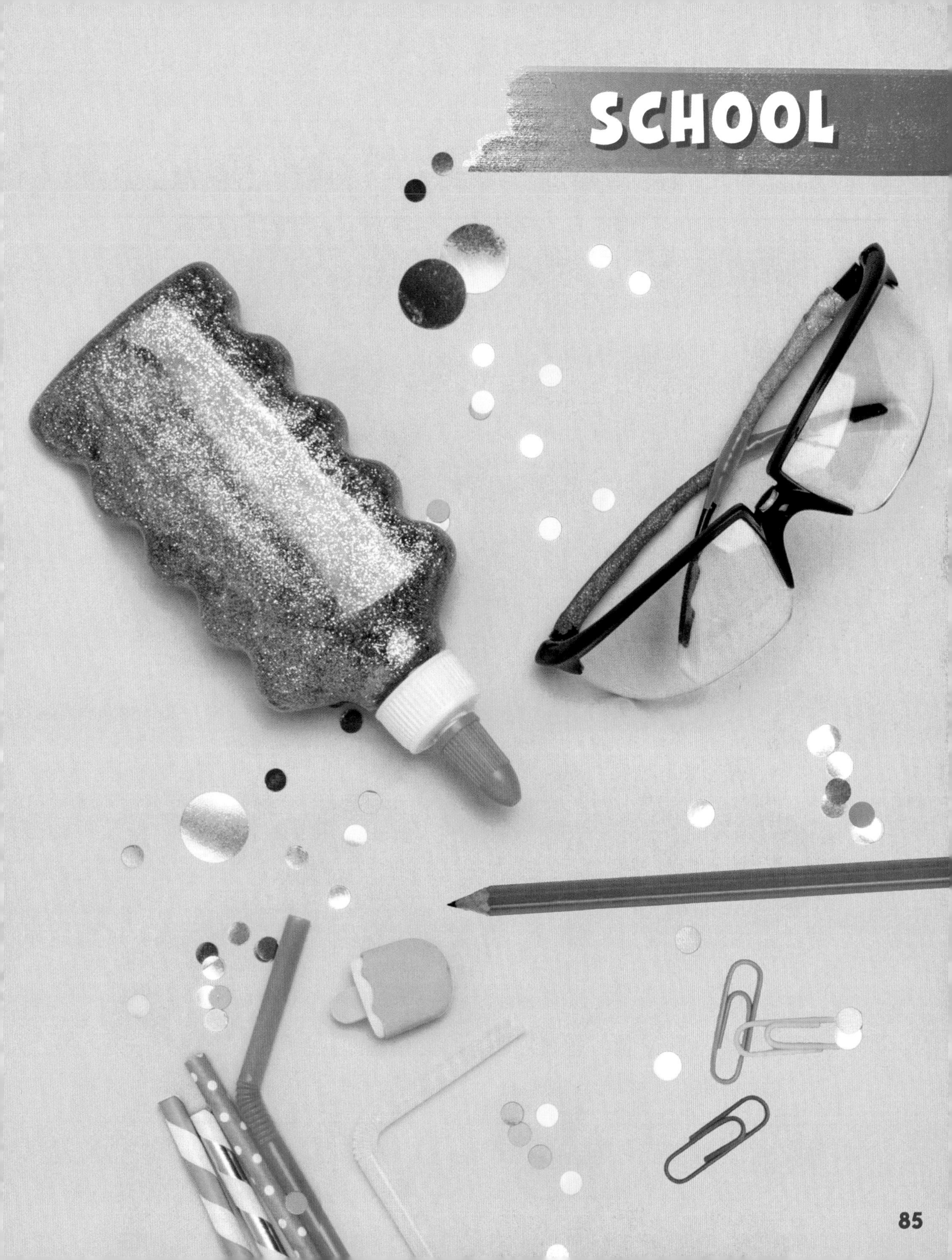

BENTO BOX

A great way to organize your snacks. This way you'll know exactly where to find each one!

MATERIALS

❑ Lunch box
❑ Tupperware of different sizes that can fit inside the lunch box
❑ Cupcake liners

1. Open the lunch box and line it with the different-size Tupperware.
2. Put some cupcake liners inside the Tupperware.

3. Fill the liners and the Tupperware with your favorite snacks.

4. Cover the Tupperware with lids.

5. Use cupcake liners to cover your remaining snacks.

6. Add an eating utensil and a napkin to your lunch box. Then close it up and head on out!

Bento box lunches can fuel your creativity, which is so important as a scientist. Cut two small circles and a mouth out of seaweed to turn that lump of rice into a smiley face. Any meal can be a masterpiece if you let your creativity run wild!

Making can be a pretty messy business, but it's always good to start with everything in its place. You can use this bento box model in other ways, like storing your decorations. Instead of using food, add beads, jewelry, or stickers to each of the compartments. Just make sure you don't accidentally switch this box with your lunch!

RAINBOW HIGHLIGHTER

Because rainbows are so happy!

MATERIALS
❑ Yellow highlighter
❑ Pink highlighter
❑ Blue highlighter

1. Open the yellow highlighter.
2. Take the pink highlighter and leak it onto one side of the yellow highlighter.

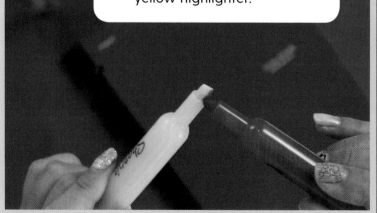

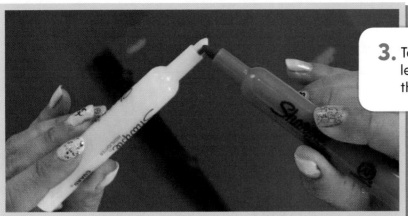

3. Take the blue highlighter and leak it onto the other side of the yellow highlighter.

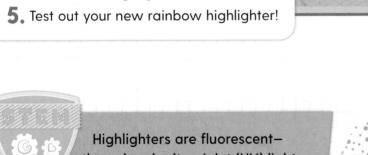

4. When you're done, the yellow highlighter will absorb the colors of the other highlighters.

5. Test out your new rainbow highlighter!

Highlighters are fluorescent—they absorb ultraviolet (UV) light, which humans can't see, and emit light we *can* see. They're like super-fast glow-in-the-dark markers.

Why stop at yellow, pink, and blue? Create your own fabulous rainbows with any color highlighters you want!

EMOJI MAGNETS

For all the feels . . .
there is an emoji.

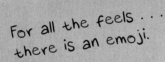

MATERIALS

- ❏ 12 round magnets
- ❏ Yellow paint
- ❏ Paint pens

1. Paint one side of each magnet yellow. Let them dry.

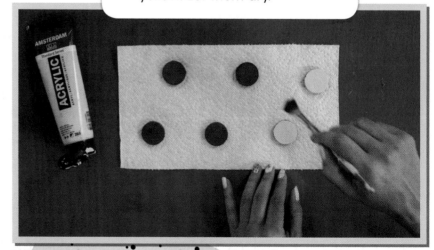

2. Use your paint pens to draw different faces on the magnets.

3. Feel free to have fun!

4. When you're done, you'll have enough emoji magnets to show the whole world how you feel.

STEM

Think magnets will stick to your stainless steel fridge? Think again. Magnets stick best to iron and nickel but won't stick at all to copper, aluminum, or the chromium that makes steel shiny.

Have a different favorite emoji? Like, oh, I don't know, a waffle emoji? Just use a different magnet! Put a different emoji on your locker every day, depending on how you're feeling. And if you want to get really creative, you can find square, rectangle, or heart-shaped magnets at a craft store.

EDIBLE GLUE

Sticky and sweet and utterly delicious.

1. Roll up the glue stick as far as it will go.
2. Twist off the glue.

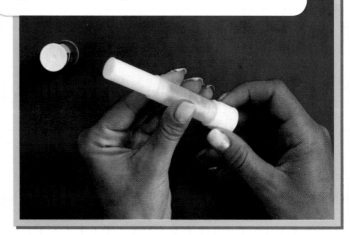

MATERIALS
- ❏ Glue stick
- ❏ Assorted Starburst candies

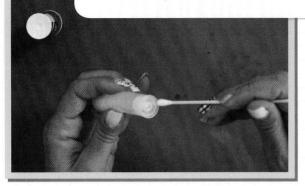

3. Clean the glue stick container thoroughly with soap and water.

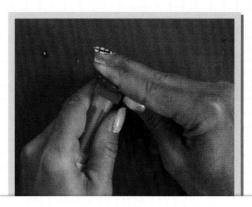

4. Unwrap a Starburst and place it on top of the glue stick.
5. Using something hard (like a bottle cap), press the Starburst into the glue stick.

6. Peel off the excess Starburst.
7. Repeat steps 4–6 until the glue stick is full.

People used to make paste from nothing more than cornstarch and water, but it's stickier with some sugar and vinegar. Use your candy-based glue to decorate cakes.

For a mini version of this hack, use a tube of ChapStick instead!

COLOR-CHANGING THERMAL NOTEBOOK

Is it hot today or is it just me? Better check my notebook! What?

MATERIALS

- ❏ Notebook
- ❏ Black acrylic paint
- ❏ Thermal pigment
- ❏ Hot glue
- ❏ Sequins

1. Paint your notebook cover black.

2. Let the paint dry completely.

3. Paint a thick layer of thermal pigment over the cover and let it dry.

4. Hot glue some sequins on for the final touch.

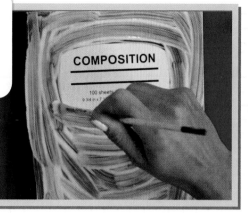

COMPOSITION

100 sheets

5. Aim a hair dryer at the cover and watch it change colors!

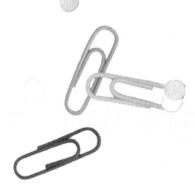

Liquid crystal paint has the same material as liquid crystal display (LCD) televisions. Like slime, liquid crystals are a non-Newtonian fluid. They can flow like liquids while stacking like solids!

This hack works on more than just notebooks! How about on your phone case, calendar, or wallet? Don't want to use sequins? Try using colorful tape around the edges instead!

Thanks for hacking along with me! I hope you made some amazing projects—and came up with some original ones of your own.

If you want more, subscribe to my channel at **youtube.com/goldieblox**. New videos are uploaded every week. Tell me in the comments section which hacks you've completed—or improved!

Until next time, Hackers!